33x10/10 - 2/11
32x2/13 - 1/14

MM

BARRON'S

Hartmut Wilke

Tortoises and Box Turtles

Photography: Uwe Anders

Illustrations: György Jankovics

CONTENTS

THE TYPICAL TORTOISE

- Solitary by nature.

- Hard shelled but very sensitive to touch.

- Loves to bask in the sun.

- Has a beak instead of teeth.

- Can be tamed.

- Has a keen sense of smell.

- Learns quickly.

- In the wild, may live for more than 150 years.

- Many species hibernate.

Strictly speaking, the term *tortoise* applies only to the true tortoises, members of the family Testudinae. In nonscientific usage, however, the term often refers to other terrestrial turtles as well. Because the land-dwelling species generally require similar care in captivity, this book describes several terrestrial turtles, including the box turtles, and uses the word tortoise in its broader sense.

In the time of the dinosaurs, when turtles first inhabited the earth, the climate was much warmer than now. The turtles and tortoises of today are still more or less adapted to these conditions. Therefore, their natural habitat lies primarily in the

world's tropical and subtropical regions where sunshine is not lacking. However, some species have been able to adapt to the changing seasons of North America, Europe, and Australia by hibernating during the cold of winter. If you choose a tortoise as a pet, you should definitely know all about its basic needs and see that they are met. Doing so will allow the creature to thrive.

DECISION MAKING

1 Are you allergic to animal hair? No problem—research has shown that tortoises do not trigger allergies in humans.

2 Many tortoises enjoy fresh outdoor air in the summertime. Do you have a yard or garden your pet tortoise could use?

3 If not, do you have a patio or balcony (facing south or southwest) where you can build a comfortable tortoise box?

4 Many tropical species of tortoises are very delicate and should be kept indoors except during very warm and sunny weather (see "Profiles," starting on page 10).

5 Providing a suitable indoor environment is very important for your tortoise's health. Tropical species that do not hibernate spend most of their lives in a terrarium.

6 Do you have an appropriate place for an indoor terrarium? Drafts and constant vibrations (from stereo systems, for example) are harmful to tortoises (see page 21).

7 Do you have access to a cold cellar or unheated basement for overwintering your tortoise? Temperature fluctuations in attics, garden sheds, greenhouses, and balconies make them unsuitable hibernacula.

8 A sick tortoise must be treated by a veterinarian familiar with tortoises' special treatment needs. You should locate such a specialist ahead of time so that your tortoise can get help in an emergency.

9 Do you have other pets? Keep in mind that dogs and cats see tortoises as prey. Friendships can develop, but they rarely occur. In addition, rodents will not hesitate to try their teeth on a tortoise. Snake owners should be aware that tortoises might carry pathogens that may be fatal to snakes.

10 Plan ahead to find someone who can take care of your tortoise in case you are sick or away from home (see page 38).

One Tortoise or Two?

✔ Tortoises are by nature solitary creatures, and they do not necessarily need a partner.

✔ In the wild, tortoises may be more sociable during the mating season, but these are opportunistic pairings that do not last for long.

✔ If you plan to breed tortoises, you need at least one of each sex.

✔ If you breed them, you also need a terrarium of appropriate size, facilities to keep the two tortoises separated when they are not getting along, a way to incubate the eggs, and a separate terrarium for raising the young.

✔ Choosing a breeding pair from among young tortoises can be a matter of luck. When young, males and females are difficult to distinguish. If two young males live in the same habitat, one may start to bully the other as they reach maturity.

✔ Males and females of different species may tolerate each other and may even provide each other amusement or exercise (possibly including tussles as they compete for the same food). Only rarely, however, does their mating produce offspring, even in closely related species. Furthermore, for the sake of species protection, avoiding crosses between different species is preferable.

PREPARATION AND PURCHASE

Tortoises were highly valued in many ancient cultures. Even today, many find these creatures fascinating. Before you keep a tortoise as a pet, however, you should be familiar with the habits and needs of these interesting primeval reptiles.

The History of Tortoises

Tortoises come in all sizes, from the immense to the relatively tiny. On the Seychelles and the Galapagos Islands, tortoises have evolved into massive creatures that weigh as much as 450 pounds (200 kg) but are so strong that they move easily even over steep and rugged lava fields. Other tortoises may be only 4 inches (10 cm) from tip to tail. Some of these smaller species, like the box turtles, have developed a shell that closes up tight, enabling them to protect their limbs from predators.

As long as 180 million years ago, at a time when neither birds nor mammals existed, turtles and tortoises lived on the earth. The oldest turtle fossils from the Mesozoic era have been found in Germany, at the edge of the Harz Mountain range. These turtles had grown more than 20 inches (0.5 m) long. The mouth of the fossilized turtles contained small, knobby teeth overgrown by the gums. Vestiges of teeth could also still be clearly identified on the jaws. Today's turtles no longer have teeth. Instead, they have horny jaws with jagged edges they use to bite off food.

The male Three-toed Box Turtle has a distinctive red iris.

The shell of turtles and tortoises has also undergone a wide variety of adaptations during the course of evolution. The very flat shell of the African Pancake Tortoise is reduced to a thin, resilient layer that affords no protection. To hide from its enemies, this tortoise must squeeze into narrow crevices in its rock-strewn habitat. Other tortoises, such as the box turtles and Hinge-backed Tortoises, have hinged upper or lower shells. After pulling in their head and limbs, these tortoises can close up their houses tightly.

Also worth mentioning are the sea turtles. They have a flat shell and legs that have evolved into paddles, enabling them to swim and dive extremely well in the ocean. The largest and heaviest sea turtle, the Leatherback Turtle, has only the vestige of a shell in the form of seven bony ridges that support its leathery hide.

---

*Important note: On pages 12 and 17 (indicated by asterisks), there are four breeds of tortoise or box turtle that are extremely delicate when kept in North America. The publisher does NOT recommend keeping them as pets in the United States and Canada.

Hermann's Tortoise.

Margined Spur-thighed Tortoise.

Hermann's Tortoise
Testudo hermanni

Size: Up to 8 inches (20 cm).

Distribution: Greece, Italy, France, Spain, and the former Yugoslavia.

Habitat: Open, semiarid plains with scattered rocks and shrubs; abundant sun and partial shade. The tortoise hides in caves.

Behavior: Active by day, likes to climb and dig.

Care: Terrarium and outdoor enclosure; air temperature 64°F (18°C) at night to 79°F (26°C) in the daytime. Add a basking light for hot spot temperatures of 95–100°F (35–37°C). Can be kept outdoors from June to August and, with additional heat source, also keep outdoors in May and September. On cool days, use an overhead spot lamp (see page 21).

Diet: Leaves, grass, and hay. Prefers dried foods to fresh. No meat.

Hibernation: Not required unless breeding planned.

The hatchling works hard to emerge from its shell.

Margined Spur-thighed Tortoise
Testudo marginata

Size: Up to about 12 inches (30 cm).

Distribution: Southern Greece; has also been introduced into Sardinia.

Habitat: Sunny slopes thickly vegetated with grass and shrubs through which the tortoise traces narrow paths.

Behavior: Active by day, likes to climb and dig; lively if given proper care.

Care: In the United States, this tortoise tends to do poorly in captivity. Terrarium and outdoor enclosure; air temperature 64°F (18°C) at night to 79°F (26°C) in the daytime. When possible, keep outdoors from June to August. On cool days, use an overhead spotlight (see page 21). In autumn and spring, before and after any hibernation, keep in a terrarium.

Diet: Leaves, grass, and other greens; in autumn, also hay; remember to provide water.

Hibernation: Only for those in peak condition.

Special notes: Hermann's tortoise and margined spur-thighed tortoises can interbreed. For species protection, avoid such crossbreeding. Instead, substitute a suitable mate of the same species.

TORTOISES

Mediterranean Spur-thighed Tortoise.

Horsfield's Tortoise.

Mediterranean Spur-thighed Tortoise
Testudo graeca

Size: Up to about 10 inches (25 cm).

Distribution: Southern Europe, Iran, Egypt, Libya, and Morocco; four subspecies exist.

Habitat: Open, semiarid and rocky plains; abundant sun and light shade. Hides in caves.

Behavior: Active by day, likes to climb and dig; lively if given proper care.

Care: Terrarium and outdoor enclosure; air temperature 64°F (18°C) at night to 79°F (26°C) daytime. With no additional heat source, keep outdoors from June to August; with additional heat source, keep outdoors also in May and September. If daytime temperatures are cooler, supplement the sun's warmth with an overhead spotlight (see page 21). Before and after hibernation, keep in a terrarium.

Diet: Leaves, grass, and other greens, and in autumn, also hay; remember to provide water.

Hibernation: Only for those in peak condition.

Special notes: The African species need considerably higher temperatures and usually do not hibernate.

Horsfield's Tortoise
Testudo horsfieldii (Agrionemys horsfieldii)

Size: Up to 8 inches (20 cm).

Distribution: East of the Caspian Sea, in deserts and mountains from Iran to Pakistan.

Habitat: Regions with dry, sandy, and loamy soil; scattered rocks; grass and bushes.

Behavior: Active by day; lively; climbs and digs.

Care: Terrarium and outdoor enclosure; air temperature 64°F (18°C) at night to 79°F (26°C) in the daytime. With no additional heat source, keep outdoors from June to August; with additional heat source, keep outdoors also in May and September. If daytime temperatures are cooler, use an overhead spotlight (see page 21). Before and after hibernation, keep in a terrarium.

Diet: Leaves, grass, and hay; remember to provide water.

Hibernation: Yes, for those in peak condition.

Tender young leaves, like these from a wild grapevine, are a tasty treat for tortoises.

Bell's Hinge-backed Tortoise.

Home's Hinge-backed Tortoise.

*Bell's Hinge-backed Tortoise
Kinixys belliana

Size: Up to 8 inches (20 cm).

Distribution: Madagascar and central and southern Africa.

Habitat: Open, arid plains with dry, sandy to gravelly soil and scattered grass and bushes.

Behavior: Active by day.

Care: Delicate. Terrarium and outdoor enclosure; air temperature 68°F (20°C) at night to 86°F (30°C) in the daytime. Keep in outdoor enclosure only during really nice summer weather.

Diet: Grasses, other greens, mushrooms, slugs, snails, earthworms, and some fruit.

Hibernation: No, although exceptions may occur; watch for the signs (see page 31).

Special note: The publisher does not recommend keeping these as pets in the United States.

*Home's Hinge-backed Tortoise
Kinixys homeana

Size: Up to 8 inches (20 cm).

Distribution: West Africa.

Habitat: Tropical rain forest with soil rich in leaves and humus.

Behavior: Active by day; may like to soak in water dish.

Care: Delicate. Tropical terrarium; humidity 70-80%; air temperature 75°F (24°C) at night to 86°F (30°C) in the daytime. Note: Do not let the soil get moldy. The air must always smell fresh. Provide good ventilation. (Don't forget the water dish!)

Diet: Grasses, greens, mushrooms, slugs, earthworms, and some fruit.

Hibernation: No.

Special note: The publisher does not recommend keeping these as pets in the United States.

Most tortoises will enjoy nibbling on fresh birch leaves, which are nontoxic.

TORTOISES

Ornate Box Turtle.

Eastern Box Turtle.

Ornate Box Turtle

Terrapene ornata

Size: Up to 6 inches (15 cm).

Distribution: At lower elevations of the United States between the western tributaries of the Mississippi.

Habitat: Fertile grassland; sandy, semidry soil with low bushes near water sources.

Behavior: Crepuscular (active in morning and evening twilight). Spends the day in hiding.

Care: Terrarium and outdoor enclosure; air temperature 64°F (18°C) at night to 82°F (28°C) in the daytime. May be kept outdoors from June to August. In autumn and spring, keep in a terrarium.

Diet: Earthworms, grasshoppers, crickets, may eat greens and puppy food.

Hibernation: May be beneficial to specimens living in the north end of the range.

Special notes: The sexes can be distinguished by eye color—the iris in the male is reddish brown; the female's is a yellowish white. This is a delicate species, even for those experienced in turtle care.

Eastern Box Turtle climbing.

Eastern Box Turtle

Terrapene carolina (four subspecies)

Size: 2–8 inches (10–21 cm) (varies among subspecies).

Distribution: Central and eastern United States.

Habitat: Damp woodlands and meadows.

Behavior: Crepuscular. Spends the day in hiding.

Care: Terrarium and outdoor enclosure; 64°F (18°C) at night, 82°F (28°C) daytime. May be kept outdoors from June to August. In autumn and spring, keep in a large terrarium. Box turtles like early morning and late afternoon sun.

Diet: Meat, greens, and mushrooms.

Hibernation: Yes, for those in the northern part of the range (see page 31).

Indian Star Tortoise.

Serrated Hinge-backed Tortoise.

The following tortoises are rarely seen in pet shops. However, captive-bred specimens are sometimes available.

Indian Star Tortoise
Testudo elegans
Size: Up to 10 inches (25 cm).
Distribution: Central and southern Indian peninsula, Sri Lanka, and Pakistan.
Habitat: Grassy, lightly forested savannas at lower elevations in mountain and hill country.
Behavior: Active by day.
Care: Semiarid terrarium with subtropical-to-tropical climate; air temperature 72°F (22°C) at night to 79°F (26°C) in the daytime. Use overhead spotlight to heat basking area to 97°F (36°C) for 5–6 hours a day. Changes in humidity have a positive effect on this tortoise's activity. To increase humidity, spray the terrarium with distilled water.
Diet: Grasses, dandelions, other greens, and fruit.
Hibernation: No, although this tortoise may have a period of limited activity in summer (4–5 weeks) during which it will be apathetic and lose its appetite (see page 33).

Serrated Hinge-backed Tortoise
Kinixys erosa
Size: Up to 12 inches (about 30 cm).
Distribution: West Africa.
Habitat: Tropical rain forest with soil rich in leaves and humus.
Behavior: Active by day.
Care: Well-ventilated terrarium with tropical climate; humidity 70–80%, air temperature 75°F (24°C) at night to 86°F (30°C) in the daytime. Do not let the soil get moldy! The terrarium must have good ventilation. Provide water and a moist corner where the tortoise can go.
Diet: Grasses, other greens, mushrooms, slugs, snails, and some fruit.
Hibernation: No.
Special note: Carapace is jointed, allowing tail end of shell to close.

The tortoise may snap up some tree leaves.

TORTOISES

Red-footed Tortoise.

Yellow-footed Tortoise.

The following tortoises are occasionally available for sale. Their adult size, however, makes them too large to be kept inside a terrarium.

Red-footed Tortoise
Geochelone carbonaria
Size: Up to 20 inches (about 50 cm), though only after 15 years.
Distribution: Tropical South America.
Habitat: Rain forest with soil rich in leaves and humus.
Care: Large outdoor enclosure with a greenhouse that offers a subtropical-to-tropical climate (relative humidity above 70%). For young tortoises, use a terrarium with tropical conditions, air temperature 75°F (24°C) at night to 86°F (30°C) in the daytime. Do not let the soil get moldy! The air must smell fresh and tangy. Provide good ventilation and a moist corner hideaway.
Diet: Grasses, greens, fruit, and a little animal protein.
Hibernation: No.

Yellow-footed Tortoise
Geochelone denticulata
Size: Up to 20 inches (about 50 cm).
Distribution: South America east of the Andes.
Habitat: Rain forest with soil rich in leaves and humus.
Behavior: Active by day.
Care: Large outdoor enclosure with greenhouse offering a subtropical-to-tropical climate (relative humidity above 70%). For young tortoises, use a terrarium with tropical conditions, air temperature 75°F (24°C) at night to 86°F (30°C) in the daytime. Do not let the soil get moldy! Always provide good ventilation and a moist corner hideaway.
Diet: Grasses and greens; rarely, fruit and animal protein.
Hibernation: No.

The Red-footed Tortoise is particularly attractive.

Leopard Tortoise.

Sub-Saharan Spur-thighed Tortoise.

Leopard Tortoise

Geochelone pardalis

Size: Up to 24 inches (60 cm).

Distribution: Central to southern Africa.

Habitat: Savannas; grassland with scattered trees and bushes.

Behavior: Active by day.

Care: Indoor terrarium only for young tortoises; adults will outgrow it. Large outdoor enclosure with greenhouse offering a subtropical-to-tropical climate; air temperature 72°F (22°C) at night to 79°F (26°C) in the daytime. Use overhead spotlight to heat basking area to 97°F (36°C) for 5–6 hours a day. This tortoise needs a cave to crawl into for hiding. Can be kept outdoors from June to August.

Diet: Grasses, greens, chopped broccoli, and rarely fruit.

Hibernation: No.

Sub-Saharan Spur-thighed Tortoise

Geochelone sulcata

Size: Up to 30 inches (75 cm), weight up to 175 pounds (80 kg). This is the largest of the world's mainland tortoises!

Distribution: Africa, south of the Sahara.

Habitat: Savanna, desert.

Behavior: Active by day. Persistant burrower.

Care: Cannot be kept in a terrarium.

Note: Hatchlings are readily available. Think about the adult size before purchasing.

"Land Turtles" That Really Are Freshwater Turtles

Although the following two species are often considered to be terrestrial, they are actually freshwater turtles. They spend much of their time on land—certainly more than other semi-aquatic species. In the wild, however, these species seek out ponds and streams. This means that you must make suitable provisions when setting up the terrarium. A dry terrarium is not appropriate.

Young Leopard Tortoises are cute, but they will outgrow an indoor terrarium.

TORTOISES

Vietnamese Leaf Turtle.

"Terrestrial" Keeled Box Turtle.

*Vietnamese Leaf Turtle
Geoemyda spengleri
Size: Up to 6 inches (15 cm).
Distribution: Southern China, Vietnam, Indonesia.
Habitat: Tropical mountain rain forests.
Behavior: Active by day.
Care: Semi-aquatic terrarium with 50–75% land area (simulate a forest floor with leaves and moist bark chips). Try providing a strong current in the water area; if the turtle seeks it out, keep the current going. A rocky bottom provides good footing. Water temperature 75–79°F (24–26°C), air temperature 75–79°F (24–26°C). This turtle can be kept in an outdoor enclosure (garden pond with a running stream) from June to August.
Diet: Omnivorous.
Hibernation: No.
Special notes: This species of turtle has a pronounced hook on its upper jaw, which it uses in climbing. This hook must not be trimmed. The turtle's feet have relatively undeveloped webs (presumably as an adaptation to fast-flowing waters). Again, the publisher does not recommend keeping these as pets in the United States and Canada.

*Keeled Box Turtle
Pyxidea mouhoti
Size: Up to 7 inches (18 cm).
Distribution: Vietnam and Laos.
Habitat: In and around waters of the tropical rain forest.
Care: Semi-aquatic terrarium. Very delicate; high mortality of wild-caught specimens; cage air temperature 73–77°F (23–25°C) and soil temperature 68–72°F (20–22°C).
Behavior: Active by day. Juveniles are primarily aquatic, while older turtles are chiefly terrestrial. They burrow into the moist, leafy forest floor and rarely bask.
Diet: Omnivorous.
Hibernation: No.
Special notes: The pronounced hook on the upper jaw is used when climbing. The publisher does not recommend keeping these as pets in the United States.

Where to Get a Tortoise

You should buy a tortoise from a pet shop or directly from a breeder.

A pet shop: You do not have to worry when buying a tortoise from a reputable pet shop. Your receipt, listing the scientific name of the tortoise, will serve as your tortoise's papers. Never buy a tortoise on the spur of the moment. Ask for the tortoise's scientific name. Find out what sort of care it requires before you buy. Ask the pet shop staff or a tortoise expert, or consult the profiles in this book. Although many types of tortoises are occasionally offered for sale, not all will do well in captivity. Furthermore, many species become quite large. Others, like the soft-shelled turtles and snapping turtles, though sometimes sold in pairs, are suitable only for solitary living quarters.

A breeder: Thanks to successful breeding practices, buying some protected turtle species is no longer difficult. Breeders often advertise in magazines for reptile and amphibian owners as well as in the specialized turtle and tortoise publications (for information, see page 62). You should visit the breeder to see how the turtles are cared for, where they are kept, and what their quarters look like. You can ask the breeder to show you the breeding stock, and maybe even your tortoise's parents. A reputable breeder will also serve as a knowledgeable resource if you have questions or problems later.

Note: If the tortoise you want is not available immediately, you may be able to order it from the breeder.

Male or Female?

If your tortoise is to be kept alone, its sex does not matter. Males and females are alike in their behavior. If you are looking for a suitable mate for your tortoise, choose from nearly full-grown or adult specimens. Otherwise, distinguishing between males and females can be difficult.

In many species of tortoises, the male's plastron is more concave than the female's. Males also usually have a somewhat longer tail, which is narrower at the base, with the vent closer to the end of the tail (see photos, page 20). In some adult tortoises, the color of the eyes is another way to determine the tortoise's sex (see page 13). When in doubt, consult an expert.

The Tortoise's Age

The age of a tortoise can be estimated readily only when it is young. If you know the tortoise's eventual adult size and if your pet is approximately one-third this large, it is about three years old.

After another three years, the tortoise will have reached about two-thirds of its adult size. However, this is only a rough rule of thumb, because how fast a tortoise grows

You cannot tell how old a tortoise is by counting the growth rings on the plates of its shell.

depends a great deal on its living conditions. Furthermore, the growth rate slows as the tortoise gets older.

Radiated Tortoises. The sense of smell is extremely important for contact between tortoises.

When to Get a Tortoise

If you are buying a tortoise (whether adult or young) that will hibernate, buy it in the summertime—not earlier than May or later than September. In autumn, determining whether an unresponsive tortoise accustomed to hibernation is about to hibernate or is ill can be difficult. If you bring home a sick tortoise and it hibernates, it will probably not survive. For the same reason, buying a tortoise just coming out of hibernation is also not advisable. If it had the beginnings of a health problem at the start of winter, the problem will only become worse after the tortoise awakens.

Species from tropical regions do not hibernate and can be purchased at any time of year. If you buy one of these tortoises, however, you should keep in mind that they are very sensitive to drafts. Tropical species must be kept warm and secure when they are moved during winter (see "Transporting a Tortoise" on page 28).

Proper Shelter

Tortoises—especially young ones—that do not receive enough light, sunshine, calcium, and vitamins can develop the bone disease known as rickets. When this occurs, the limbs and shell

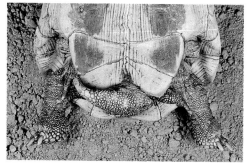

The shell of a healthy tortoise is firm but elastic. Test with gentle pressure!

The male tortoise's tail (top) is definitely longer than the female's (bottom).

become soft and deformed. To prevent this, a tortoise kept indoors needs a diet and a terrarium with some specialized modifications. The size and layout of the terrarium will help determine the quality and the length of your tortoise's life. It will not thrive in a box—it needs a spacious playground with room for sunning, exploring, and seclusion. When planning your caging, try to provide regular access to an outdoor enclosure. In any case, make the terrarium as large as possible.

To calculate the minimum dimensions for a terrarium, do the following. Multiply the length of the adult tortoise's shell (in inches or centimeters) by five; this will give both the length and width of the terrarium's base. Multiply length by width to determine the surface area needed for a single tortoise. For each additional tortoise, you should enlarge the area by one-third.

You can purchase a terrarium at a pet shop or you may find a second-hand bargain in the classified ads. A used aquarium, sold for a few dollars just because the glass is scratched or a seal is cracked, will make a perfectly good terrarium.

Setting Up a Terrarium

The ideal location for a terrarium is under a glass roof, such as in a greenhouse. Here the natural daylight enters from above, and the tortoise experiences the changing day lengths of the different seasons. For many species, this can have an important influence on readiness for hibernation or breeding.

Placing the terrarium near a large window is also fine. However, take care that the tortoise is not exposed to drafts when the window is opened. Tropical species, in particular, are very sensitive to drafts and cold. If the terrarium is in a room with no window, you must provide adequate light and heat (see page 23). Do not place a terrarium directly onto the floor or in front of the window. This exposes the tortoise to heat or cold and to drafts that can make it sick. Rather, set the terrarium onto a base, for example, a Styrofoam pad. In addition, be aware that vibrations transferred from a refrigerator or stereo equipment will disturb your tortoise.

Proper Lighting

If the terrarium is in a dark spot, you will need to provide artificial sunlight for your tortoise to exhibit normal behavior and be happy and for the terrarium plants to be healthy. Be especially aware of light conditions if the terrarium is in a basement or in a room with small or no windows.

You need to provide heat and full-spectrum ultraviolet and visible light for most species. The heat will be from a reflector fitted with a basking bulb. The ultraviolet light will be from a fluorescent fixture fitted with an ultraviolet-emitting bulb (Vita-Lite by DuroTest is one brand). Connect the fluorescent fixture to an electric timer set to mimic the natural local photoperiod. The fluorescent light will enable

TIP

Tortoise Species Conservation

The Washington Convention on International Trade in Endangered Species of Wild Fauna and Flora (CITES) provides for the protection of flora and fauna whose worldwide survival is threatened. Animals threatened with extinction may not be sold or bought without special permission. When tortoises are listed under CITES, it means that special permits are needed before the animals can be imported into the United States.

Many states protect their native tortoises, forbidding removal from the wild and prohibiting private possession and commercial trade of protected species. The Federal Endangered Species Act enforces state protection by prohibiting interstate transport and trade of any protected species. In addition, public health laws in the U.S. prohibit the sale or trade of any turtles under 3 inches (7.5 cm) in length, except for scientific purposes.

Be aware that individual states may change their regulations for specific species of turtles from time to time. Keep current on laws and regulations by calling your state fish and game agency. You have the responsibility of checking with the appropriate authorities to be sure your purchase is legal.

Checklist for a Healthy Turtle or Tortoise

For best results, evaluate a tortoise's health during the summer months. Follow the checklist given below.

Test	Observations
Shell in good condition:	*Young tortoises, up to one-third of adult size:* Shell firm and elastic, like a thumbnail. *Adult tortoises:* Shell hard and firm. All scutes (horny plates) firm and intact.
Shell in poor condition:	*Young tortoises and adults:* Shell gives way when pressed, like crust on a dinner roll (soft, not elastic). *Adults:* Firm but then changes shape, individual plates very bumpy or profile from the side very bumpy. *Plastron:* Holes in horny plate; pink, watery blisters under or in horny plate; loose or missing plates, bare (whitish yellow) bone exposed.
Skin healthy:	Outside of heavy scales on neck and legs is leathery, soft, and elastic.
Skin not healthy:	Cracked and stiff. Infested with ticks and mites.
Eyes healthy:	Clear, bright, opened wide.
Eyes not healthy:	Cornea clouded, eyes swollen; lids closed.
Nose healthy:	Dry, no bubbles, no noise when breathing.
Respiratory tract not healthy:	Bubbles at nose and mouth, opens mouth wide while craning the neck, rattles when breathing.
Claws healthy:	Firmly attached to foot with healthy nail bed, no missing claws.
Claws not healthy:	Claws loosely embedded or missing, nail bed inflamed (reddish or whitish) and/or swollen.
Movement on land:	All four legs used for forward motion, no dragging of rear legs (causes nerve damage!).
General responsiveness:	When picked up, the tortoise either moves vigorously in defense or pulls back strongly into its shell.

you to raise young tortoises if you are unable to give your pets time in an outdoor enclosure. Read all labels and ask your pet store for help before buying. Bulbs labeled as full spectrum may be only color corrected and emit little ultraviolet light. The ultraviolet light ensures healthy bone growth in your tortoise. Most ultraviolet-emitting bulbs are designed to be hung just 18 inches (45 cm) above the tank floor.

Cage Furniture

Research your tortoise's natural habitat, and imitate this biotope in the terrarium. It's important not to keep making changes, because your tortoise needs a familiar environment. Arrange roots and rocks so that the tortoise must climb over or around them. Provide inviting nooks and crannies where your pet can rest, hide, or forage for food.

Plants are not essential, but they look pretty in the terrarium. Choose sturdy, nontoxic plants such as aechmea, aloe, guzmania, sansevieria, or schefflera. Set the plants into clay pots, and cover their soil with rocks or roots. Some plants may be eaten. Container plants such as *Ficus benjamina* (weeping fig) add an attractive touch of green around the outside of the terrarium. **Note:** Do not choose poisonous plants for decoration. Never use pesticides in the terrarium.

Terrarium Equipment

A well-equipped terrarium for tortoises must provide the following:
✔ a shallow water bowl large enough for the tortoise or turtle to crawl into and that contains water at 72–75°F (22–24°C);
✔ a place to hide away at night;
✔ a warm area of sand or stone kept at 75–79°F (24–26°C) in which the turtle or tortoise can bask, with the remainder of the cage at 64–72°F (18–22°C);
✔ a corner with moist, unheated sand.

Warm zone: You can use several methods to provide the necessary warmth in the terrarium. Electrically heated rocks, available at pet shops, are the most convenient; you simply have to plug them into an outlet. Place them so that the electric cord passes directly out through the corner of the terrarium. Cover the cord with a flat rock, so the tortoise cannot dig it up and chew on it. Some hobbyists have reported that their tortoises have been burned by these "hot rocks."

Another option is to construct the following system (see illustration, page 24):

Obstacle course. Taking a tumble now and then will not hurt your tortoise.

A well-equipped terrarium with bathing pool, hiding places, and a spot for sunning.

✔ First, place a sheet of pressed cork 0.5 to 1 inch (1 to 2 cm) thick onto the floor of the terrarium to cover one-half to one-third of the surface area.

✔ On top of this, place three layers of aluminum foil, shiny side up.

✔ Onto the aluminum foil place an electric heating pad that has a thermostat (available at pet shops). It should cover about the same area as the foil. The heating pad will also heat the water basin.

✔ Place a floor tile of fired clay (terra-cotta) or concrete onto the heating pad.

✔ Next to this tile and onto the heating pad, set a water basin made of clay, porcelain, or metal. (Do not use plastic, because it might melt if an equipment failure occurs.) A good choice is a shallow rectangular ceramic dish large enough to accommodate an adult tortoise comfortably. The edge must be low so that even small tortoises can get in and out without difficulty.

Note: Young tortoises can drown in the water basin. The water should be no deeper than half the height of the shell! The pool (and the land area) should also contain rocks or roots that

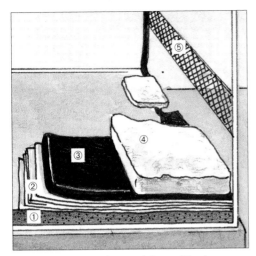

A heated area with a cork base (1), three layers of aluminum foil (2), a heating pad (3), a clay floor tile (4), and a ventilation grate (5).

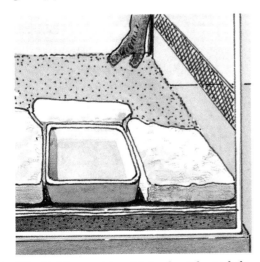

The bathing pool is set into clay tiles to help keep the area clean and then surrounded with a mixture of sand and bark.

will not shift. This will help a tortoise that is lying on its back to right itself.

✔ Now cover the rest of the terrarium floor with a half-and-half mixture of fine-grained, washed river sand and bark chips.

Note: If your tortoise eats the sand, replace it with loess, loam, or forest soil. Otherwise, the tortoises's gastrointestinal tract may become obstructed.

✔ Finally, arrange roots and rocks to add interest and variety to the terrain and give your tortoise a place to hide or sleep.

Placing the water dish atop the heating pad will increase humidity in the cage. Be prepared to move the water dish if your tortoise shows signs of stress.

An Outdoor Enclosure

If you provide an outdoor enclosure with a cold frame and an additional heat source, you can keep your tortoise outdoors from May to September.

Minimum size: At least 4 feet (1.2 m) wide and 10 feet (3 m) long.

Fencing: Set cement slabs, lawn-edging tiles, smooth wooden planks, or corrugated plastic (available from garden shops) into the ground. Take care that the tortoise cannot reach the top edge of the enclosure with its front feet, or it will climb out. Tortoises less than 4 inches (10 cm) long are easy prey for crows, jays, or hawks and need a cover made of wire mesh or netting to protect them.

Ground: Excavate to a depth of about 1 foot (30 cm). The ground must have a grade of about 2 inches per yard (5 cm per m). Leave mounds and hillocks that protect the tortoise from high waters and serve as a basking spot.

Vegetation: Sow grass and weeds (dandelions, chickweed) and add low shrubs (boxwood).

Place rocks and roots so the tortoise cannot use them to climb out.

Cold frame: At the upper end of the enclosure, in a sunny spot, install a cold frame made of plexiglass to act as a shelter. Because of the greenhouse effect, this will hold sufficient warmth even in relatively long periods of bad weather. For a doorway, you can easily cut a rounded opening in the plexiglass with a fretsaw. Locate the opening so that the tortoise will come upon it as it walks the perimeter of the enclosure.

For cold days, when the temperature in the hut does not reach 79°F (26°C), install an infrared lamp or a 60- to 80-watt lightbulb that can hang from the ceiling. (Monitor the temperature to avoid overheating!) Make the floor of the shelter from cement pavers, because they store heat well.

Note: Cold frame kits can be purchased in garden shops. You can cut the plexiglass pieces yourself and insert them into the frame kit.

Feeding spot: Even though grass and other greens are available, you will need to feed your

tortoise. A stone slab in front of the cold frame (in a shady spot) serves as a dining area and makes cleaning up food remnants from the pen easier.

Bathing spot: At the low end of the pen, install a tilted shallow pool with a drainage ditch to allow rainwater to run off so a sudden cloudburst will not drown your pet. A birdbath (made of cement or plastic) containing about 1 inch (2 cm) of water makes a suitable pool.

Fresh Summer Air on the Balcony or Patio

Even if you do not have a yard, you can give your tortoise a vacation in the fresh air.

Here is what you will need:

✔ A balcony or patio that faces south or southwest.

✔ A vented enclosure large enough to provide shade if the sun gets too hot.

✔ Protection from wind and drafts.

What to do:

✔ Build a box from squared timbers and spruce boards, about 5–6 feet (1.6–2 m) long, 2 feet (60 cm) wide, and 2.5–3 feet (80–100 cm) high (about as high as a windowsill or

The outdoor enclosure should face south or southwest. On cool days, the tortoise can retreat to the cold frame to stay warm.

*A tortoise box
on a balcony or
patio must be
protected against
drafts.*

balcony railing).
To keep the box
from rotting, use a
waterproof adhesive
and line the bottom
and lower sides with
a plastic sheet.

✔ For a partial cover,
use a plexiglass pane
about 3 feet (1 m)
wide. Have the cover
extend a little over the
front edge (for rain protection).
The box should be about 4–6 inches
(10–15 cm) lower in front than in back so that
the plexiglass pane lies at an angle. This allows
more sunlight to enter, and the rain can run
off better.

✔ To secure the cover against storms, pass
bungee cords about ³/₁₆ inch (5 mm) thick
through holes in the plexiglass panes, and
fasten them to hooks on the front of the box.

✔ Place a flat rock into a shady corner to act
as a feeding area.

✔ A birdbath of suitable size, purchased in a
garden or pet shop, can be included to make
a good pool.

✔ Now fill the bottom of the box 4 inches
(10 cm) deep with pumice (from a garden
shop). Top this with several layers of garden
or forest soil. Leave enough space at the top
so the tortoise cannot climb out over the
edge of the box. Add plants and decorations
to suit your own taste. Small shrubs from the
boxwood family work very well.

Transporting a Tortoise

Although buying your tortoise in summer is advisable, you may occasionally need to transport it in winter, for example when taking it to the veterinarian. You must be very careful when taking your pet outdoors in temperatures below 65°F (18°C). Fill a hot-water bottle with warm water at about 86°F (30°C), and place it into a cardboard box. Put your tortoise into a sack made of cotton or linen, and set it—right side up—onto the hot-water bottle. Close the box, wrap it in a blanket, and place it into a paper bag, folding the bag to close it securely. The box contains enough air to last your pet for at least an hour of cold, outdoor travel. If you are in a heated room or a warm vehicle, you can open the box to give your pet a little fresh air. Never expose a tortoise to an ice-cold draft, even for only a few breaths. Doing so can lead to serious illness.

To transport a tortoise in cold weather, tuck it into a cotton sack, set it onto a hot-water bottle, and pack it into a cardboard box.

Taking a Stool Sample

Although a newly acquired tortoise may seem to be fit as a fiddle, it might have a worm infestation or a bacterial, viral, or amoebic infection. Inspect it thoroughly (see table, page 22), and have a stool sample analyzed by a veterinarian. The veterinarian can give you special contain-ers for stool speci-mens; in an emer-gency, empty film canisters will do. Take a stool sample every day for three days and have each ana-lyzed. Add a drop of water to each con-tainer so the sample will not dry out and lose its value for testing. The oldest sample must be no more than five days old when submitted for analysis.

Until then, keep the stool samples in the refrigerator to pre-vent the growth of mold, which would also make them unfit for testing. The tor-toise must remain in quarantine until it can be officially declared healthy.

Veterinarians can supply containers for stool specimens.

The Quarantine Terrarium

The quarantine terrarium is important for a sick tortoise. It is also useful if two tortoises are not getting along. In some cases it can serve as hibernation quarters (see page 33).

A simple aquarium made of glass, about 24 × 20 × 20 inches (60 × 50 × 50 cm), makes a good quarantine terrarium. Provide a food dish, a water dish, and a hiding place, such as a board resting on two bricks. Line the walls at the back with black plastic, and place a board across the top to provide some darkness. As in the permanent terrarium, of course, some technical equipment is needed (see pages 24–25). A source

Because cleanliness is important, the quarantine terrarium is simple, even spartan.

of warmth is particularly important.

Note: A black plastic mortar pan (from the hardware store) with a capacity of 12–65 gallons (about 50–250 liters) will also work as quarantine quarters. Line the bottom with newspaper. Add a water dish and a hiding place—a piece of tile for a small tortoise or a board resting on two bricks.

First, a Bath!

Before putting the tortoise into quarantine, you should give it a good bath. At the same time, once more inspect it thoroughly for injuries (see table, page 22). Place the tortoise into a good-sized bowl of warm water about 79°F (26°C) that is not too deep. Be sure the tortoise can hold its head above water level; you can allow it to drink. The warm water will slowly loosen any remaining bits of dirt from its body. A bath about 10 to

20 minutes long is generally adequate. Dry the tortoise. Water evaporating from its surface could cause it to lose body heat, stressing the tortoise further. When you put the tortoise into its quarantine terrarium, it will probably crawl right into its hiding place.

Rub-a-dub-dub, tortoise in a tub.

PROPER CARE AND FEEDING

Tortoises are quiet pets. You will need to keep an eye on your pet's appearance and behavior to be sure that it is healthy. Although the most essential requirement is appropriate shelter, a proper diet and correct handling are also important.

What You Need to Know About Hibernation

Tortoises native to moderate climate zones, such as the northern United States and Europe, need a period of relative inactivity during winter. In the wild, food is scarce, and a tortoise's body does not stay warm in cold weather. To conserve energy, the tortoise rests, some hibernate. Its metabolism, breathing, and heart rate become slower, and movement slower. This allows the tortoise to survive the winter cold. This rest period also has a positive effect on the reproductive behavior of adult tortoises. If your tortoise belongs to a hibernating species, you should make the necessary provisions for it to hibernate.

It is important to know where your specimen originated. It may be that not all populations of a particular species hibernate; for instance, spotted tutles from Massachusetts certainly hibernate each winter. Spotted turtles from Florida don't need to hibernate, although they may enter into brief wintertime periods of dormancy.

Clambering over obstacles as it forages for food helps to keep a tortoise fit.

Some species, such as the Horsfield's Tortoise, undergo a comparable period of relative inactivity during the summer in their native habitat. This estivation period allows the tortoise to survive the hot dry seasons when food and water are scarce. Even in moderate climates, pet tortoises may sense this need, especially if kept outdoors during a very hot summer.

The length of your tortoise's hibernation period depends on the native habitat of its particular species. You will need to do a little research. When the average daytime temperatures in your tortoise's homeland stay below about 64°F (18°C), your pet must hibernate. When the temperatures rise and remain above this temperature, the hibernation period is over. As a rule, the normal hibernation period for a tortoise is three months.

On the other hand, even where temperatures do not become prohibitively cold, toirtoise and box turtle species slow their activities and may actually hibernate for 30, 60, or 90 days. In this case, it would seem that the cessation of activity is caused more (or at least as much) by waning day lengths than by lowered ambient temperatures.

Seven Golden Rules
for a Healthy Tortoise

1 Never let a tortoise crawl around on the floor indoors. Cold floors and drafts are the most common cause of serious ailments in tortoises.

2 Give your tortoise a varied diet of healthy foods that contain the nutrients it needs. A tortoise may seem to relish white bread and milk, but such foods can make your pet fat and may lead to liver damage.

3 Do not expose your tortoise to a draft from an open window even if the weather is warm outside. The tortoise may develop fatal eye and lung inflammations.

4 Provide the right kind of shelter. A cardboard box is not a good home for a tortoise. Your pet needs an environment that offers suitable temperatures, sunlight or ultraviolet light for basking, interesting and varied terrain, and water for bathing.

5 Part of the terrarium floor must be heated. Tortoises are cold-blooded creatures whose body temperature varies with the temperature of their surroundings. If the temperature is too low, they become ill.

6 Four weeks before you start to overwinter your tortoise, carefully evaluate its health, and have stool samples tested for worms. A tortoise that is not healthy might not survive the hibernation period.

7 Do not let your tortoise hibernate by burying itself outdoors or in a garden shed. It would be defenseless against rodents and other predators, and a long cold winter would be too hard on your pet.

Signs That It Is Ready to Hibernate

In October, as the length of the day and the strength of the sun decrease, tortoises become more sluggish and have little appetite. They stay in hiding for longer periods, often burying themselves head first in the darkest corner. When this happens, even if some days are still warm, stop feeding your pet. It needs time before it hibernates to digest the food it has already eaten and to empty its bowels completely.

For a Horsfield's Tortoise or Star Tortoise, the estivation period likewise begins with less active behavior and a loss of appetite. If you observe these signs, first check carefully to determine whether your tortoise is ill; you may want to consult a veterinarian. If your tortoise is healthy, it is probably getting ready for its summer rest.

Note: Tortoises need to hibernate even during their first year of life. However, you should weigh your hibernating tortoise every five to six weeks. (This will not wake it up.) If a young tortoise's weight decreases by more than 15 percent during hibernation, you have cause for concern. You should go ahead and wake the tortoise (see page 34).

Ways to Overwinter a Tortoise

✔ Well before hibernation, preferably in August, have your tortoise checked by a veterinarian. This will allow sufficient time to treat any health problems that need attention.
✔ To begin the overwintering process, bathe the tortoise (see page 29) for two or three days in a row in warm water about 75–79°F (24–26°C) for 10 to 20 minutes. This will allow the tortoise to empty its bowels completely.

Weigh your tortoise at regular intervals before, during, and after hibernation.

✔ Then turn off the heat and light in the terrarium. Keep the room temperature below 64°F (18°C) for two to three days.
✔ When the tortoise becomes relatively sluggish, place it into its hibernation box (see page 37).
✔ Do not forget to weigh your tortoise before it hibernates (for small pets, use a postage scale). Weigh it again every five to six weeks. Adult tortoises normally lose 10 percent of their body weight during hibernation, and young ones may lose 15 percent. If the weight loss exceeds this, wake the tortoise, and take it to the veterinarian.
✔ The room temperature in the basement where you keep the hibernation box can vary between 32°F and 54°F (0–12°C), but it must not rise above 54°F (12°C) for more than one week or the tortoise will awaken too soon.

Note: While it hibernates, the tortoise must not be fed. Weighing your pet will not disturb it. In a dry basement, the fill material in the hibernation box may dry out. If necessary, add a small amount of water in a corner at the

level of the garden soil. Be sure the water penetrates into the soil and does not create a muddy spot.

Young tortoises, in particular, are liable to develop serious health problems if they become dehydrated.

How a Tortoise Wakes Up

At the end of the appropriate hibernation period (see page 31), take your tortoise out of its basement hibernation box and place it into its shelter in a quarantine terrarium. At first, it will not respond; do not be concerned. Set the terrarium into a relatively warm room of 68–72°F (20–22°C) and wait for it to emerge.

Now you have some jobs to do:

✔ Bathe the tortoise in warm water about 75–79°F (24–26°C), to which you have added 2 tablespoons (30 ml) of salt per quart (l).

✔ Let the tortoise drink all it wants; then place it into its terrarium. Adjust the heat and light to the appropriate levels (see species profiles, beginning on page 10).

✔ Offer fresh food and water every day. Your tortoise may take up to a week before it begins to eat again.

Winter is coming—time for a tortoise to tuck in for a long nap.

If Your Tortoise Will Not Hibernate?

If your tortoise is one of the species that hibernates, and it is from the northern part of its range, you should try to give it the winter rest it needs. This is true even if your tortoise is older and has not been overwintered in years. Follow the steps described on page 33. If the tortoise still remains active, go ahead and put it into the basement in the hibernation box you have prepared (see page 37). Wait for a week. If it has not yet settled into hibernation, observe it carefully and weigh it more often. If your pet loses 10 percent of its body weight within two to three weeks, it is not strong

enough to hibernate. You must take it to the veterinarian. A healthy tortoise will go into hibernation within two to three weeks even if it has not hibernated in years.

What If It Wakes Up Too Soon?

One day you may check on your hibernating tortoise only to find that it has already emerged and is looking around with a lively air. If this happens, first weigh it. If it has lost too much weight (see page 33), take it to the veterinarian. Otherwise, follow the steps described above.

If your tortoise shows normal behavior, takes a good drink, and starts to eat within the

expected time, you probably do not need to
consult a veterinarian.

*In spring, the tortoise wakes and emerges
from its winter quarters.*

Housing Tortoises Together

Tortoises by nature are solitary creatures and
will not miss not having a companion (see page
7). If you want to keep more than one, though,
you must take certain precautions:

✔ Be sure to provide a hiding place for each
tortoise in the terrarium.

✔ The basking area must also be spacious
enough to prevent scuffles. Having one or two
more sunning spots and hideaways than
tortoises is better.

✔ A long-established inhabitant will defend its
territory against a newcomer. If this happens,

the old-timer should be sent to quarantine
quarters for about two weeks. During that
time, the new tortoise can make itself at home
and become less readily intimidated.

If the tortoises continue to do battle, or if
one tends to stay in hiding, you will have no
choice but to separate them permanently.

Note: One way to help tortoises learn to get
along is to keep them in a spacious outdoor
enclosure during the summer months. This
makes it easier for the tortoises to stay out of
each other's way.

Grooming for Tortoises

When given the right shelter and a healthy diet, a tortoise needs very little cosmetic care.

Tweezers are useful for removing splinters or bits of loose skin.

Ticks can be easily removed with a special tick puller.

Have the veterinarian show you how to trim your tortoise's claws with special clippers.

If a tortoise spends the summer outdoors, ticks may lodge in folds in the head and legs. These parasites can be easily removed with special tick pullers purchased from outdoor suppliers or some drug stores. Which way you turn the tick to pull it out does not matter.

A tortoise's claws will not wear down as they should if the ground underfoot is too soft. Too much animal protein in the feed also leads to excessive claw growth (and doming of the scutes on the carapace). The long claws hinder the tortoise's movement and must be trimmed with special clippers (see illustration, top right). These are sold at pet shops. Having your veterinarian teach you how to trim the claws is best.

The horny beak around the mouth may grow to be too long if the tortoise's food is too soft or contains too much protein. The horny excess must be filed off by a veterinarian. The keeled box turtle *Pyxidea mouhoti*, among other species, naturally has a hook on its upper jaw, which aids it in climbing. This must never be trimmed.

The shell actually needs no cosmetic care, though it may become somewhat dull and colorless as the tortoise grows older. You may rub a

To trim the claws, hold the foot firmly between your thumb and forefinger against a flat surface. With your other hand, apply the clippers to trim at an angle.

Even tortoises kept indoors year-round may get ticks, for example from forest soil spread on the terrarium floor.

very small amount of petroleum jelly or hoof oil into the shell. Then carefully rub the shell dry with a soft cloth.

Note: If the application is too thick, the horny layer will not be able to breathe. The grease also attracts dust, and the tortoise will look worse than before.

Basic Tortoise Care

	Tortoises	Equipment and Routine Care
Shelter	Terrarium (dry); also outdoor enclosure; possibly hibernation box. Enclosure is simple; technical equipment needed (see page 23).	Hibernation box (see below) needs fresh bedding every year. Inspect and repair technical equipment (especially electrical cords).
Care of Shelter	Cleanliness is essential (see page 46).	Mixture of bark chips and sand must be replaced every 2 to 3 months. Wash roots and rocks.
Feeding	Chiefly herbivorous, some omnivorous.	Offer fresh greens, hay, vegetables, and some insects.
Common Errors in Care	Keeping tortoise on the floor leads to eye and lung inflammations.	Monitor health carefully all year long (see table, page 22).

The Hibernation Box

A tortoise can safely overwinter in a hibernation box, preferably located in a cool basement at 32–54°F (0–12°C). The hibernation box measures 28 × 28 inches (70 × 70 cm) and is 32 inches (80 cm) high. It is made of boards loosely fastened together so that air can penetrate into the box.

Fill the bottom of the box to a depth of about 4–8 inches (10–20 cm) with moist lava rock or pumice (from a garden shop). Next place a 4-inch (10 cm) layer of moist garden soil. Finally, fill the box to about 4 inches (10 cm) below the edge with peat moss and leaves that are dry but not too dry. Place the tortoise onto this layer. It will dig its own way into the lower layers. Finally, cover the box with cheesecloth or wire mesh.

This hibernation box provides a safe place for your tortoise to spend the winter.

VACATION CARE

Tortoises are happiest in their own familiar environment. You should not take them with you on your travels. Plan ahead to find a reliable person to care for your tortoise in your home.

Checklist for Vacation Care:
✔ *Equipment: Explain how to tell if something is wrong. Demonstrate how to perform a simple inspection. What if the timer or other electric devices are not working properly? Show what to do for simple repairs. If possible, provide the name and address of a knowledgeable person who can help.*
✔ *Feeding: Write down how much and what to feed. Specify how often and when to feed.*
✔ *Behavior: Describe normal behavior and any peculiarities of behavior. Is it the mating season? Is it almost time for the tortoise to hibernate or to lay eggs? Is the tortoise just coming out of hibernation? Describe possible illnesses. Leave the address and telephone number of a veterinarian or other expert who can be called on for advice.*

Healthy Diet, Healthy Tortoise

Tortoises are essentially herbivores. In their natural habitat, grasses, weeds, and bushes offer a wide variety of leaves, blossoms, and fruits. The plants and soil harbor insects, caterpillars, and snails, which meet the tortoise's need for animal protein.

Your pet tortoise likewise needs a varied diet if it is to stay healthy. True, tortoises will happily eat bananas, white bread or rice soaked in milk, or lettuce. If they become accustomed to these, tortoises will decline any other food. In the long run, however, such a lopsided diet is not good for them. They will get fat without getting the nutrients they need, and they may get sick and even die. Instead, give your tortoise a variety of healthy foods from the start.

Blossoms, Greens, Vegetables, Fruit

Forage for greens in your yard or garden. Choose from dandelions, daisies, buttercups, and many other flowers.

Wild greens may include dandelions, chickweed, yarrow, buckhorn or broadleaf plantain, orache, coltsfoot, parsley, dill, chervil, clover, or meadow grass (in autumn, also alfalfa and hay, always served with a drink of water). Grass and hay are rich in fiber and should always be the main portion of the diet!

Note: Avoid greens and vegetables that have been sprayed with weed killers or pesticides. Do not feed your tortoise poisonous plants.

You can offer your tortoise a wide variety of vegetables, preferably minced. Try carrots, kohlrabi, radishes, beans, and peas (including tubers and tops) as well as tomatoes and cucumbers. Feeding your tortoise lettuce and other leafy vegetables is also a good idea.

All tortoises like fruit—raspberries, strawberries, bananas, pineapple, apples, and pears—

especially when it is overripe and sweet to the taste. However, do not feed your tortoise sweet fruit exclusively. With its high sugar content, fruit can ferment in the intestines and promote the proliferation of parasites.

Note: Tortoises have a keen and refined sense of taste. Unless they are very hungry, they will first sniff their food thoroughly to decide if they like it. Tortoises tend to prefer their favorite foods and spurn the other healthy choices you offer. You can outwit your pet tortoise by mincing the other foods and mixing them into the food it likes best.

Dietary Supplements

Vitamins, minerals, and trace elements (available in pet shops or from a veterinarian) are essential for a tortoise's healthy development.

A feed rack can be useful, especially if you have several tortoises.

These are provided in commercial diet supplements, such as ReptaMin or Osteoform, which are generally sold as powders. Every tortoise, small or large, needs one pinch of this powder twice a week. Mix the powder thoroughly with your tortoise's favorite food.

Calcium is especially important for shell and bone development in growing tortoises and for formation of the eggshells in adult females. Calcium is available as a special preparation in pet shops, or you can meet your tortoise's needs by adding ground eggshells to the diet.

Standard Foods for Your Tortoise

Season	Dietary Staples
Spring	Greens—chickweed, dandelions, daisies, plantain, grass, fresh nontoxic tree leaves; earthworms and crickets.
Summer	See Spring.
Autumn to winter (do not feed during hiberation)	Romaine lettuce, kohlrabi leaves, leafy hay, autumn leaves that have not turned brown; earthworms and crickets.
	Feed foods fresh or prepared as an aspic (see page 41).
Year-round	Dietary supplements in small amounts. Twice weekly, one pinch of a mineral/vitamin mixture (ReptaMin or Osteoform, see page 39); two to three times weekly, calcium (ground eggshells) and grated carrots.

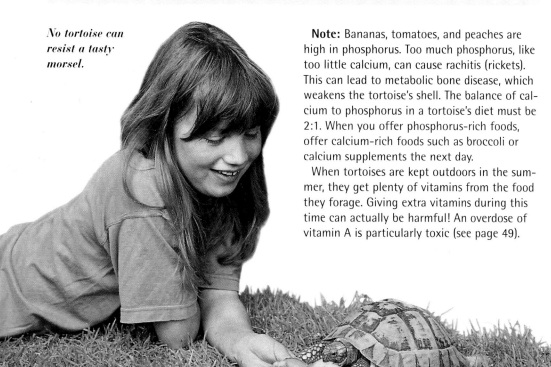

No tortoise can resist a tasty morsel.

Note: Bananas, tomatoes, and peaches are high in phosphorus. Too much phosphorus, like too little calcium, can cause rachitis (rickets). This can lead to metabolic bone disease, which weakens the tortoise's shell. The balance of calcium to phosphorus in a tortoise's diet must be 2:1. When you offer phosphorus-rich foods, offer calcium-rich foods such as broccoli or calcium supplements the next day.

When tortoises are kept outdoors in the summer, they get plenty of vitamins from the food they forage. Giving extra vitamins during this time can actually be harmful! An overdose of vitamin A is particularly toxic (see page 49).

A Special Recipe

This complete tortoise food can be made in bulk and frozen in portions for later use.

Ingredients: Eighty-five to 90 percent plant material of varied content (field greens, romaine lettuce, high-fiber vegetable leaves, and chopped vegetables such as carrots, kohlrabi, or radishes). Ten percent fat-free ground beef. Five percent cooked corn meal or brown rice. Eggshells.

Preparation: Rinse plant material and eggshells well under running water. Puree them in a high-speed mixer, add a little water to form a thin mash. Add remaining ingredients, mix well, and heat the mash to 175°F (80°C) (check the temperature with a food thermometer).

For each generous quart (L) of mash, add 1 level teaspoon (5 ml) of mineral/vitamin supplement (see page 39).

Stir the mash constantly while it cools to 140°F (60°C). Now add a high-quality gelatin powder (from the grocery store), following package directions to make aspic. (Inferior aspic powder will not set the food properly, and the food will disintegrate when thawed.) Pour the food into a shallow pan or dish. After it sets, cut the aspic into daily portions, place it into plastic bags, and freeze.

Checklist
Feeding Guidelines

1 Unfortunately, no hard-and-fast rule says how much a tortoise should eat. However, a healthy tortoise often eats more than is good for it. Watch your pet carefully, and try to develop a feeling for how much food it needs. Weighing a tortoise at regular intervals will help you to know whether it is eating too much.

2 Feeding a tortoise twice during its daily active period is best. Keep fresh drinking water available at all times.

3 If the folds of a tortoise's skin bulge out of its shell when it draws in its legs, it is too fat. Reduce the amount of food by about 30 to 40 percent until the fat deposits under its skin are no longer evident.

4 Make changes gradually. To introduce a new healthy main food, mix a little in with the preferred food, then gradually increase the proportion.

Breeding Tortoises

If given care appropriate to the species, tortoises will reproduce even in captivity. Remember to register your tortoises with the local natural protection authorities before breeding them; otherwise, you won't receive the necessary documents for the eventual offspring. You must give the female a healthy diet and vitamin and mineral supplements to permit her to form strong eggs. Provide a nursery area and food for the hatchlings. Once the young begin feeding, you can find new homes for the ones you do not wish to keep.

Sexual Maturity

European tortoises are sexually mature when they are three to five years old. Many other

The mating season for many tortoise species is between the end of April and the end of May.

species reach reproductive age when they are five to eight years old. However, the ability to reproduce depends not only on age but also on the growth rate and the young tortoise's environment. Favorable living conditions and rapid growth promote earlier sexual maturity.

Tips for Successful Breeding

✔ If your tortoise belongs to a hibernating species (see pages 10–17), be sure hibernation occurs each year.

✔ If possible, keep a breeding pair in an outdoor enclosure during the summer months. The chance of successful breeding is best in a

The male may make hissing or whistling
noises during mating.

warm and pleasant summer. If your tortoises
live in a terrarium year-round, cycling your
tortoises gives a better chance at success.

✔ Tortoises that do not hibernate should be
separated for one to two months before you
plan to breed them (keep them where they
cannot see, hear, or smell each other). Tortoises
that hibernate naturally experience this
separation during the winter.

✔ Three months before you want them to mate,
decrease the artificial daylight provided by the
overhead spot lamp and other terrarium lighting

to just six hours a day. After two months,
increase the lighting gradually over three to four
weeks, to a maximum of 10 to 12 hours daily.

✔ When you decrease the hours of light, also
reduce the air and water temperature by about
8–10°F (4–5°C) below the upper limit given in
the species profile (see pages 10–17). Turn off
additional heat sources such as spotlights and
underground heating mats.

✔ As you extend the hours of daylight,
gradually increase the air and/or water
temperature over three to four weeks. During
the final week, turn on the overhead spotlight
and/or the heating pad, adding an hour a day.

✔ During the final week, spray the terrarium
and the tortoises twice a day with a plant
mister, using softened water. This increases the
humidity. Higher humidity, along with the rising
temperature, helps to trigger the mating urge.

✔ When you give your tortoises fresh, tender
food while increasing the temperature, they
will sense that spring has come and it is time
to begin their courtship behavior (see page 56).

Fertilizing the Eggs

You should know what happens when your
tortoises mate according to plan.

The male has already formed his sperm
during the previous summer and stored
it during hibernation.

The female has likewise established her eggs
in the summer. Their development reaches
completion in springtime, after the winter rest.
Before the shell is formed, the eggs are fertilized. This does not require mating each time;
many females can store sperm for up to four
years. Even if no male is around in the mean-
time, a female might still lay fertilized eggs
after one to three years.

Artificial Incubation

Tortoises will bury their eggs in the terrarium if the sand is warm, slightly moist, and at least as deep as their shell length. Depending on their size, some European tortoises lay as many as 30 eggs a year. After the eggs are laid, you should remove them to safety so that the tortoise will not damage them in the confined space of the terrarium. Mark the top of each egg with a soft lead pencil. They must not be turned for the rest of the incubation period. Otherwise, the yolk will crush the embryo, and it will die. Although many species deposit all the eggs at once, others do so at intervals of five to thirty days. Numbering the eggs will help you know when to expect hatchlings to emerge.

The incubation chamber consists of a clear plastic container, half filled with slightly moist vermiculite (from the hardware store) or damp builder's sand. Bury the eggs halfway in the vermiculite. Then close the lid of the container. The humidity inside will rise to the 100-percent level that is needed. Lift the lid once a day, and fan a little fresh air into the container. To keep condensation on the underside of the lid from

Even in more northern latitudes, tortoises will bury their eggs outdoors. However, the climate is not mild enough to ensure that the eggs will hatch.

A ready-made incubation chamber (available at pet shops) works well for tortoise eggs.

dripping onto the eggs (which can kill the embryos), tilt the container, setting one edge on a matchbox or similar object so the condensation can run off the lid at an angle. Now place the container of eggs into a room where the ambient temperature is 82°F (28°C). The incubation chamber described on the next page offers ideal temperatures.

The Ideal Incubation Chamber

The following arrangement is ideal. Place two bricks into a plastic terrarium, as shown. Add water to just below the top of the bricks. Set the plastic container of eggs onto the bricks. Heat the water to 82°F (28°C) with a simple aquarium heater. The temperature can vary slightly, perhaps 2–4°F (1–2°C) higher or lower.

Cover the aquarium with a pane of glass. Tilt the aquarium with a small wedge made of wood to allow the condensation under the glass to run off.

The baby tortoises hatch after about 90 days (for European Tortoises and many Box Turtles). Other species (such as the Leopard Tortoise) may take as long as 400 days.

Caring for Baby Tortoises

Once the baby tortoises have emerged, you may leave them in the incubator for a

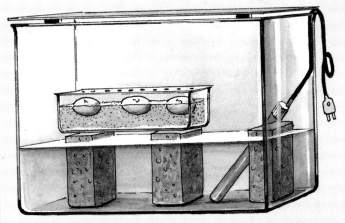

This plastic terrarium, half-filled with heated water, provides ideal temperatures for incubating tortoise eggs.

few days until the yolk sac on the navel has shriveled and fallen off. Of course, this requires an incubator of adequate size. After this, hatchlings are raised separately from their parents. Hatchlings need the same living conditions—for example, temperature and food—as the adult tortoises. However, about a week will pass before the baby tortoises eat. Their metabolisms need that time to adjust from digesting the

yolk to digesting solid food. Mince their food somewhat smaller so that the young tortoises can grasp it easily. Provide the necessary calcium and vitamins (see page 39). Be careful not to give an excess of vitamins—too much is as harmful as too little.

Tortoises can take one to three days to hatch. During this time, the hatchlings must not be disturbed.

Preventive Care

Most health problems in tortoises kept as pets can be traced to improper care. At the top of the list of errors are exposure to drafts (see page 21), inadequate heat sources (see page 24), improper diet, and vitamin deficiencies or overdosage (see page 49). Negligence of hygiene can also lead to serious ailments.

Cleanliness Is Essential

Water dishes and the damp sand around them are perfect holding grounds for stomach and intestinal parasites, their eggs and larvae, and amoebas and bacteria of all kinds. In the wild, tortoises roam over wide areas and never again encounter the parasites that they excrete. In the terrarium, this is necessarily otherwise. Unless scrupulous cleanliness is maintained, the tortoise will reingest its pathogens as it eats and drinks. As the cycle continues, parasites and their eggs and larvae grow and multiply in the tortoise's body until it becomes really ill.

Scrub the water dish and change the water every day, and keep the soil around the dish dry. One way is to cover the soil with flat stones heated from below (see page 24).

Change the sand around the bathing pool often (every four to eight weeks, as needed). Tortoises like to defecate in the water. If this happens, change the water immediately.

Tortoises and Your Health

Amoebas and many other parasites live in the bodies of tortoises and other cold-blooded animals. However, these parasites are unable to survive in the human body, which maintains a constant internal temperature of about 98.6°F (37°C). For this reason, the risk of transferring disease from your tortoise is very slight. If you keep your tortoise free of worms, have its stool samples tested for parasites twice a year, keep its living quarters properly clean, and wash your hands after handling your tortoise or the terrarium, your tortoise poses no risk to your health.

Common Health Problems

Your tortoise cannot use its voice to let you know if it is sick or in pain. You must watch your pet carefully. Changes in behavior, such as apathy or loss of appetite, or external symptoms, such as swollen eyelids, indicate that your tortoise may be sick. You should take it to the veterinarian at once.

Diarrhea

Symptoms: Loose stools.

Possible causes: Improper diet, protozoal or fungal infection, worms.

Treatment: If no blood is in the feces and the tortoise is otherwise lively, first adjust its diet. Give no fruit. Reduce the amount of greens. Increase the proportion of dry food, such as leaves and hay. Instead of drinking water, offer chamomile tea or black tea (steeped for ten minutes). If no improvement occurs within two or three days, you must take the tortoise to the veterinarian. Do not forget to bring a fresh stool sample.

A little exercise on the way to dinner does a tortoise good.

Changes in Urine

Symptoms: In most tortoises, the urine is a clear, aqueous substance containing white, mucous flecks of crystallized uric acid. Abnormal urine is viscous. In advanced stages of illness, the trace of white mucus is not seen. Later, small stones can be found in the urine.

The tortoise is less lively than usual. Its joints, including those in the hind legs, are swollen.

Cause: If a tortoise does not drink enough water, its urine will become more concentrated. Greater amounts of uric acid will precipitate, forming crystals of increasing size. To conserve water, the tortoise's urine becomes thicker and thicker.

In spite of the protective mucus in the urine, eventually the cell lining of the renal tubules and anal bladder is irritated by the crystal nee-

As cold-blooded creatures, tortoises need regular basking to soak up the sun's warmth.

dles and becomes inflamed. Bacteria and protozoa can proliferate. Protein floccules, dead cells, and crystals form particles of increasing size, which block more and more renal corpuscles. The kidneys can no longer eliminate urea, which is toxic to cells, and uric acid, which causes gout. Toxic substances accumulate in the tortoise's body. Bladder stones or gout may develop, often accompanied by painful swelling of the joints.

Treatment: Take the tortoise to the veterinarian immediately. If left untreated, these illnesses are very painful and ultimately fatal. They can be prevented if the tortoise bathes

TIP

Caring for a Sick Tortoise

✔ A sick tortoise should be moved to a quarantine terrarium (see page 29). This will keep its companions healthy, prevent contamination of the terrarium with pathogens or parasite eggs, and keep sand from sticking to any body parts treated with ointment.

✔ Heat lamps and ultraviolet light: Be aware that a sick tortoise may linger too long under the heat lamp or ultraviolet light, and this may lead to overheating. Watch your pet carefully, and move it out of the hot spot if necessary. A tortoise that spends too much time under a heat lamp may become dehydrated; place it near the water dish.

✔ Hygiene: Scrupulous cleanliness in the terrarium is especially important when a tortoise is sick (see page 46).

several times a week. This allows it to take in plenty of water, which flushes the kidneys.

Respiratory Distress

Symptoms: With extended neck and gaping mouth, the tortoise makes cheeping, moaning, or snoring sounds. In between, it lowers its head in fatigue.

Possible causes: Lung infection, constipation, difficulty laying eggs (see page 49), gas in the stomach or intestines, bladder stones or uric acid calculus (preventing evacuation of the anal bladder), edema caused by kidney or heart disease.

Treatment: Do not add additional warmth! This would raise the tortoise's metabolism, which can be acutely life threatening! You should take your tortoise to the veterinarian at once for diagnosis and treatment.

Note: Fungal, bacterial, or herpes infections can cause the mouth to be coated with a mucous layer that inhibits breathing. Herpes is usually fatal. Only immediate quarantine, sanitary measures, and disinfection can save the other tortoises.

Swollen Eyes

Cause: Foreign bodies in the eye, injuries, drafts.

Treatment: Only by a veterinarian, who will rinse the tortoise's eyes clean with a small syringe and may prescribe an eye ointment.

Shell Injuries

Cause: Usually accidents.

Treatment: Superficial abrasions of the horny layer are harmless. However, if the wound is so deep that it reaches the bone, the tortoise must be taken to the veterinarian, who will remove the infected tissue and treat the bone wound daily.

Gray and White Skin Patches

Cause: Simple fungal infections

Treatment: Since poor water quality is a major cause of fungal growths, check the water your tortoise is drinking. Acriflavin, available in aquarium and pet stores, will often eradicate infections when added to the water. If growths persist, consult a veterinarian.

Mineral Deficiency

Symptom: An affected tortoise commonly eats sand or gravel in large quantities.

Possible cause: A mineral deficiency.

Treatment: Provide adequate minerals in the diet (see page 40). If the tortoise continues to eat sand and gravel, serious and possibly fatal obstructions in the gastrointestinal tract can develop.

Vitamin A Poisoning

Symptom: Shedding until the skin is raw.

Treatment: Only by a veterinarian. The tortoise must be kept very clean (to decrease the risk of infection) and fed well. Screen to protect against flies in the terrarium. Gently coat the wounds with healing ointment. Avoid using vitamin A preparations for several months.

Vitamin D$_3$ Poisoning

Symptoms: The tortoise's shell becomes soft with bleeding at the seams between scutes.

Treatment: Veterinary attention is needed.

Handle the tortoise very gently. Provide regular mineral supplements. Do not allow access to sand and gravel. Grind boiled eggshells, and sprinkle them over the tortoise's food. Avoid using vitamin D$_3$ preparations, and provide regular ultraviolet light (see page 23).

Difficulty Laying Eggs

Symptoms: Unsuccessful digging and unproductive straining while laying eggs.

Possible causes: Both mineral deficiencies and hormone deficiencies can cause this problem. Other possible causes include an egg that is too large, malformed eggs, a kinked or twisted oviduct, obstruction by sand, injury to the cloaca, or a bladder stone.

Treatment: Only a veterinarian can determine what is causing the tortoise to have difficulty laying eggs. Get immediate assistance!

Tomatoes are high in phosphorus, which must be balanced with an adequate calcium intake. Otherwise, the tortoise's shell may become soft.

BEHAVIOR AND ACTIVITY

Although many species of tortoises have adapted well to living in the care of humans, and generations have been bred in captivity, tortoises are still wild creatures. To understand a tortoise properly, learning about its natural behavior and activity is essential.

Body Language

Tortoises are usually silent. They cannot express their moods and feelings with their voices. You may hear hisses from a male during mating (see page 57) or noisy breathing from a tortoise with a serious respiratory ailment (see page 48). For the most part though, you will know whether your tortoise is doing well or not by watching its behavior.

✔ Pacing back and forth or climbing up the terrarium walls: A tortoise may cruise endlessly along the wall of its enclosure as if looking for a way out. Instead, it may go to a corner and try to climb out over the edge. This may mean that the tortoise is not happy in its surroundings. Review the guidelines for keeping a tortoise of this species (see pages 10–17).

Note: If a tortoise has just moved into its terrarium, it may simply be curiously investigating its territory. After a day or two, however, the tortoise should have calmed down.

✔ Digging in the ground: If your tortoise keeps scraping at the ground with its hind legs and if

Fresh dandelions are among a tortoise's favorite snacks.

its size is between half-grown and adult, you may have a female who is trying to lay eggs. This behavior can even be observed when there is no earth to dig in. For example, if you place the tortoise onto a smooth surface, it will still scrape and scratch. If this happens, you should immediately provide a suitable place for the tortoise to deposit her eggs (see page 44).

✔ Stretching out flat on all fours: The tortoise extends its extremities, including its head and tail, as far as it can out of its shell. The head usually rests flat on the ground, eyes closed. You will see this behavior especially outdoors in the sunshine and under the overhead spot lamp in the terrarium. Your tortoise is sunbathing.

Caution: If your tortoise spends all day in this position under the heat lamp or ultraviolet lamp, you should be concerned! Pick up the tortoise to see if it actively assumes a defensive posture. If its reaction to being disturbed seems to be less vigorous than usual, it is probably sick. You must take it to the veterinarian. Also be aware of the danger of overheating (see page 48).

✔ Standing tall, legs extended, head held high: Your tortoise is curious and wants to get a good look around. Tortoises also defecate in this position.

✔ Pulling in the head and legs: If the tortoise suddenly pulls in its head and legs, it has been alarmed and does not want to be disturbed.

✔ The tortoise raises its forelegs to mount round objects such as large stones, the toe of your shoe, or even another male tortoise: Your tortoise may be a male with an urge to mate. In the absence of a suitable partner, he is treating these objects as substitutes, perhaps mistaking them for a female. A male tortoise and an unreceptive female will flee such advances in haste.

✔ A tortoise burrows into hiding in its cave or corner and stops eating: If this happens in autumn, the tortoise may be showing signs of preparing to hibernate. Horsfield's Tortoises also exhibit this behavior before estivation, a period of limited activity in the heat of the summer (see page 33). At other times of year, such behavior can also indicate that the tortoise is ill.

The Senses

The sense of smell is highly developed, leading a tortoise unerringly to a suitable mate and to its feeding spot. The smell of a particular food is a critical factor in determining whether a tortoise will like it.

Vision is very keen, enabling tortoises to detect food and enemies from afar. For example, a Hermann's Tortoise can spy a yellow dandelion, one of its favorite foods, from a great distance. When nearby, however, it tends to follow its nose to the food. Many tortoises can also recognize a familiar person from far away.

Hearing is less acute. Tortoises hear low-pitched sounds best. You may be able to entice your tortoise to approach by calling it using a deep voice or by playing low notes on a musical instrument.

A tortoise also senses vibrations (footsteps, falling rocks) in the ground. The vibrations are conducted through the legs and shell to the inner ear. Tortoises do not have an external ear; the eardrum lies directly below the skin. For this reason, identifying the ear is often difficult. The ear is located slightly behind the jaws and is often covered by leathery skin or by scales.

The Tortoise's Shell

A tortoise's most striking feature is its shell. For the most part, the shell consists of living material that can be injured. Bony plates constitute the supporting structure of the shell, which is made of areas of ossified skin fused together with parts of the vertebrae, ribs, and shoulder girdle. The shell is thus an integral part of the tortoise's skeleton. This vaulted bone structure is covered by a membrane of connective tissue.

This layer is very sensitive—anyone who has been kicked in the shin knows how sensitive the area is. The shell is protected only by the horny shield plates. These horny plates, the *scutes,* are the only parts of the shell made of dead tissue, comparable to that of a human's fingernails.

All's well—the Box Turtle cranes its neck in curiosity.

Note: The individual scutes are joined by growth areas, usually lighter in color. Here, the horny layer is much thinner and offers little protection. These regions are highly sensitive. They should not be scratched, probed with a fingernail, or scrubbed with a brush.

Many tortoise shells have growth rings on the scutes. These give information about the shell's growth spurts. However, you cannot tell how old a tortoise is by counting the rings.

The shell of a tortoise grows more bumpy with age, and the scutes become thicker. However, the scutes wear down uniformly as the tortoise rubs against roots, thorns, and stones in its wanderings or as it burrows into the ground. As long as a tortoise is healthy, it will not lose entire scutes.

Hinged joints are another distinctive feature of tortoise shells, as seen in Box Turtles (see page 13). This modification carries the shell's protective function to amazing perfection. Normally—for example, in the case of Hermann's Tortoise—the tortoise pulls its head and all four legs into its shell. The box turtle, however, can raise the front and rear sections of its plastron like a drawbridge, closing the shell up tight and offering complete protection all around.

Other tortoises have similar mechanisms. For example, the Hinge-backed Tortoises have a jointed carapace.

The horny beak: Instead of teeth, tortoises have jaws with sharp horny edges they use to grind and shred plant and animal matter. In certain species, the tip of the upper jaw is elongated; it serves as a climbing aid (see profiles, pages 10–17).

Danger threatens—time to close down tight.

TIP

A Deformed Shell

Be wary of purchasing young or half-grown tortoises whose shells are not evenly rounded but, instead, are quite bumpy, with individual bones or scutes forming rounded cones. You may be told that these are members of a very rare species. Of course, that is ridiculous. More likely, these are deformed tortoises suffering from malnutrition; they may also have metabolic disorders. Do not buy a tortoise like this under any circumstances.

Note that certain species of tortoises, like the Star Tortoise, have nicely rounded shells when they are young but develop quite pronounced horny pyramids on the individual scutes in advanced age. This is not a sign of illness.

Understanding your pet tortoise is easier if you can interpret its behavior correctly.

 This is what my tortoise is doing.

 What does it mean?

 Here's what to do!

 The tortoise is getting a drink.

 It's thirsty.

 Provide a shallow water dish so your tortoise can drink easily.

 Climbing over an obstacle.

 Maybe it is looking for food.

 Do nothing— exercise is healthy!

 All four legs are extended.

 This tortoise is sunbathing.

 Be sure your tortoise gets plenty of sunshine.

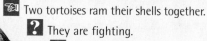 Two tortoises ram their shells together.

 They are fighting.

 If the tussling continues, you will have to separate them.

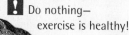

👁 Mouth opened wide.

❓ Something may be bothering it.

❗ Inspect your tortoise carefully.

☝ Standing tall on hind legs.

❓ The tortoise is defecating.

❗ Leave it alone.

 Male and female ff at each other.

 This is part of the ting ritual.

 Be prepared for eggs d hatchlings.

👁 Topsy-turvy tortoise.

❓ The tortoise flails its legs to turn itself right side up.

❗ You probably do not need to help.

👁 The tortoise digs a hole.

❓ It is ready to lay eggs.

❗ Provide an incubation chamber (see page 45).

👃 Head held high.

❓ Something is in the wind!

❗ Perhaps a tasty treat?

The claws: A tortoise's claws grow like your fingernails. They will wear down as the tortoise moves about. They grow slowly, unless the tortoise eats too much animal protein in its diet. In that case, the claws will not wear down as fast as they grow. This is dangerous, because claws that are too long may become snagged in cracks and possibly even be torn from their beds. This could result in serious inflammation that will need veterinary attention. Be sure to provide a hard substrate in the terrarium and outdoor enclosure so the claws will wear down properly.

Note: Both the horny jaws and the beak will continue to grow throughout the life of a tortoise, so be sure to watch them. If they grow too long, they must be trimmed or filed down by the veterinarian (see page 36).

The horny jaws are sharp enough to cut and crush even tough stalks.

How Tortoises Mate

A male tortoise with the urge to mate is constantly on the prowl for a female. Any object that looks even remotely like another tortoise will attract him for a closer inspection. If he encounters a female tortoise of the same species, he will recognize a suitable mate in part by sniffing, for the odor differs from species to species. Once a male has found an eligible female, he circles closely around her. Sooner or later, the female will stop to observe her suitor. Now, he will bite her front legs to make her draw them and her head into the protection of her shell. Naturally, he expects that she will not close the rear of the shell as well. If she does, he will ram his shell against hers to make her move and start the ritual again. If she cooperates and is ready to mate, the male mounts her from the rear and deposits his sperm inside her. He may make hissing, whistling, or grunting noises while he does this.

Note: The female tortoise may remain unresponsive or a male may have an excessive sex drive. The male may pester and nip at the female until she is injured or pursue her so aggressively that he prevents her from eating. In that case, separate the two tortoises for a few weeks.

A sexually mature female tortoise may lay eggs even though they have not been fertilized by mating. If your tortoise is scratching at the ground with her hind legs, make sure the terrarium has a deep layer of sand, or place her into a separate sandbox. Otherwise, she will have difficulty depositing her clutch, and the consequences can be life threatening (see page 49).

Checklist
Activities

1 Provide an environment that stimulates your tortoise's senses.

2 If your tortoise likes to climb, lay down a few stout branches wide and flat enough that the tortoise can creep with ease from one end to the other.

3 Create plenty of hideaway nooks in the terrarium. Build an obstacle course of stones and roots for your pet to crawl around and clamber over.

4 Hide food tidbits around the terrarium to sharpen your tortoise's sense of smell and encourage it to roam and forage.

5 Do not keep changing the terrarium layout; this can be unsettling to tortoises. They need familiar territory where they know their way around.

Although they are not exactly cuddly pets, many tortoises seem to enjoy being rubbed on the head. This one is stretching its neck for more.

If you are looking for lots of playing and cuddling, a tortoise is not the right pet. On the other hand, a tortoise owner can spend many fascinating hours observing the creature's behavior. Give it interesting challenges; stimulation and activity are good for your tortoise's health. Furthermore, the more time you spend interacting with your

Taming a Tortoise to Your Touch

Food is the most important element in the life of a tortoise. This means that the best way to entice your tortoise to come to you and be tamed is to provide it with a tasty snack.

Observe your pet to see what foods it likes best—a slice of banana, a dandelion blossom, a bit of tomato. Take the treat between your thumb and forefinger, and hold it out to your tortoise. The tortoise will first sniff cautiously at the food, which also smells a little like your hand.

Then it will take a few tentative nibbles. Try not to make any sudden movements now, or you will startle your pet and make it wary of you. Usually, a tortoise soon learns to associate your hand with something good to eat.

Later you can try a more advanced trick. Put a tidbit onto your wrist (palm up). Hold your open hand out in front of your tortoise like a ramp, and let it scramble up to reach the tempting treat.

Note: Do not wash your hands with perfumed soap before handling your tortoise. The perfume will mask your own individual odor, and the tortoise will not recognize you.

A tortoise that has learned to trust you will eat right out of your hand.

tortoise, the more it will learn to trust you. Tortoises can become tame to your hand, and they may even learn to come when called.

Note: For any of the tricks described on these pages, you must let the tortoise decide what it wants to do. The guiding rule is to take advantage of the tortoise's natural curiosity. Use your imagination, and always reward your pet with a tasty treat when it does what you want. Picking up a tortoise, rolling it over, and carrying it around do not qualify as entertainment or exercise.

Taming your pet tortoise to your touch can be very useful when you need to groom it, for example, to remove a tick. It will be less likely to squirm and struggle. Your tortoise voluntarily extending its limbs will be helpful, enabling you to examine areas of its skin that would otherwise be tucked away out of sight.

The tinkling of this little bell may be too high a tone for the tortoise to hear it.

Responding to Sounds

Tortoises are best able to hear low tones. You might be able to teach your tortoise to come when you ring a bell, for example, or play deep notes on the piano or another musical instrument. Tortoises have even been known to respond to their owner's voice as if it were a dinner bell. Use patience, and do not forget that the best reward is an edible one! Most of all, do not be disappointed if your tortoise does not learn this particular trick. Each tortoise has its own personality, and many simply will not respond to bribery.

"The way to the heart is through the stomach." A tender morsel will entice even the most timid tortoise.

*The reward for proper
care is a healthy tortoise.*

Useful Addresses

California Turtle and Tortoise Club
P.O. Box 7300
Van Nuys, CA 91409

Desert Turtle Preserve Committee
P.O. Box 463
Ridgecrest, CA 93555

National Turtle and Tortoise Society
P.O. Box 66935
Phoenix, AZ 85082

The New York Turtle and Tortoise Society
163 Amsterdam Ave., Suite 465
New York, NY 10023

Another Resource

You can ask questions of your pet store owner as well as the faculty of any local university that offers herpetology courses.

Literature
Useful Books

Bartlett, R. D. and Patricia. *Turtles and Tortoises.* Hauppauge, NY: Barron's Educational Series, Inc., 1996.
Ernst, Carl H., et al. *Turtles of the United States and Canada.* Washington, DC: Smithsonian Institution Press, 1994.
Ernst, Carl H. and R. W. Barbour. *Turtles of the World.* Washington, DC: Smithsonian Institute Press, 1989.

Useful Magazines

Reptile and Amphibian Hobbyist
One TFH Plaza
Neptune City, NJ 07753

Reptiles
P.O. Box 6050
Mission Viejo, CA 92690

About the Author

Dr. Hartmut Wilke studied marine biology and fisheries science at the Universities of Mainz and Hamburg, Germany. He did his doctoral research on diseases in fish. From 1973 to 1983, he was the director of the Exotarium at the Zoological Garden in Frankfurt am Main, Germany. Since 1983, he has been the director of the Vivarium Zoological Garden in Darmstadt, Germany. One of his areas of specialization is reptile breeding. He has more than 20 years of experience in the care of turtles and tortoises.

About the Photographer

The photographs in this book were taken by Uwe Anders, except for those by Reinhard (page 11, top left; page 14, top right; and page 15, top right).

Uwe Anders has a degree in biology and has been active for many years as a freelance nature photographer and a cameraman for nature film productions. He writes articles about nature, and he lectures at various institutions about nature photography and travel photography. His photographs appear in several pet owner's guides published by Barron's Educational Series.

About the Artist

György Jankovics, a graphic artist, has illustrated many guides for pet owners and gardeners.

Acknowledgments

The author and the publisher wish to thank Mr. Lutz Jakob for sharing his practical experiences from 35 years of turtle care, and Dr. Renate Keil for the chapter on "Common Health Problems."

Important Note

The electric equipment described in this book for use with terrariums (pages 21 to 26) must be of UL-listed design and construction. Keep in mind the hazards associated with the use of such electric appliances and wiring, especially near water.

The use of an electronic circuit breaker that will interrupt the flow of electricity if damage occurs to appliances or wiring is strongly recommended. A protective switch, which must be installed by an electrician, serves the same purpose.

Photos

Front cover: Horsfield's Tortoise (large photo); young Hermann's Tortoise (small photo).
Back cover: Radiated Tortoise.
Page 1: Eastern Box Turtle.
Pages 2–3: A Hermann's Tortoise takes a drink.
Pages 4–5: Two Horsfield's Tortoises feast on apples and tomatoes.
Pages 6–7: Young Hermann's Tortoise.
Page 64: Hermann's Tortoises.

English language edition ©Copyright 2000 by
Barron's Educational Series, Inc.
Translated from the German by Celia Bohannon.
©Copyright 1998 by Grafe und Unzer Verlag GmbH,
Munich, Germany

Original German title is *Landschildkröten*

All inquiries should be addressed to:
Barron's Educational Series, Inc.
250 Wireless Boulevard
Hauppauge, NY 11788
http://www.barronseduc.com

Library of Congress Catalog Card No.99-048583
International Standard Book No. 0-7641-1181-7

Library of Congress Cataloging-in-Publication Data
Wilke, Hartmut, 1943–
 [Landschildkröten. English]
  Tortoises and box turtles / Harmut Wilke ;
 photography, Uwe Anders ; illustrations, György
 Jankovics.
   p. cm.
 ISBN 0-7641-1181-7
 1. Turtles as pets. 2. Box turtles as pets. I. Title.
SF459.T8 W48   2000
639.3'92–dc21   99-048583

Printed in Hong Kong
9 8 7 6 5 4 3

1 Can a tortoise drown in a garden pond?

Yes. Tortoises cannot swim. Construct a fence around the pond to keep your tortoise safe.

2 Can I put my tortoise into the attic to hibernate?

No. The temperature variations (freezing, heat from the sun) are too extreme.

3 Will allowing a tortoise to roam freely indoors hurt it?

Tortoises are very sensitive to drafts and catch cold easily. Even on a heated floor, there may well be drafts.

4 Do most species of tortoise hibernate?

Those species native to areas where winter temperatures fall below 60°F (15°C) usually hibernate.

5 Can tortoises of different species mate and have offspring?

Yes, if the species are closely related. For example, Hermann's Tortoise and Margined Tortoises can interbreed. For species protection, such crossbreeding should be avoided.